VERBAL REASONING

WORKBOOK

An imprint of Om Books International

LETTER QUIZ

Can you figure out the answers to these questions?

If you know the letters of the alphabet, this is going to be easy.

A	B	C	D	E	F	G	H	I	J	K	L	M
1	2	3	4	5	6	7	8	9	10	11	12	13
N	O	P	Q	R	S	T	U	V	W	X	Y	Z
14	15	16	17	18	19	20	21	22	23	24	25	26

Name a fruit that begins with the fourth vowel.

orange

Which letter sounds like the name of a body organ?

______

Which letter sounds like the name of an insect?

______

Which letter sounds like the name of a vegetable?

______

Which letter sounds like the name of a tool?

______

Which letter sounds like the name given to a group of people standing in a line?

______

RIDDLES WITH LETTERS

All these riddles have Jig confused. Help him solve them.

All the answers are five-letter words.

I walk on sand in the desert.

c a m e l

I am a vegetable that will make you cry.

I tell you what time it is.

I give you a lot of wool.

I am a red fruit.

You write with me on a blackboard.

SWEET AND SOUR

Complete the sentences by unscrambling the words and filling in the blanks.

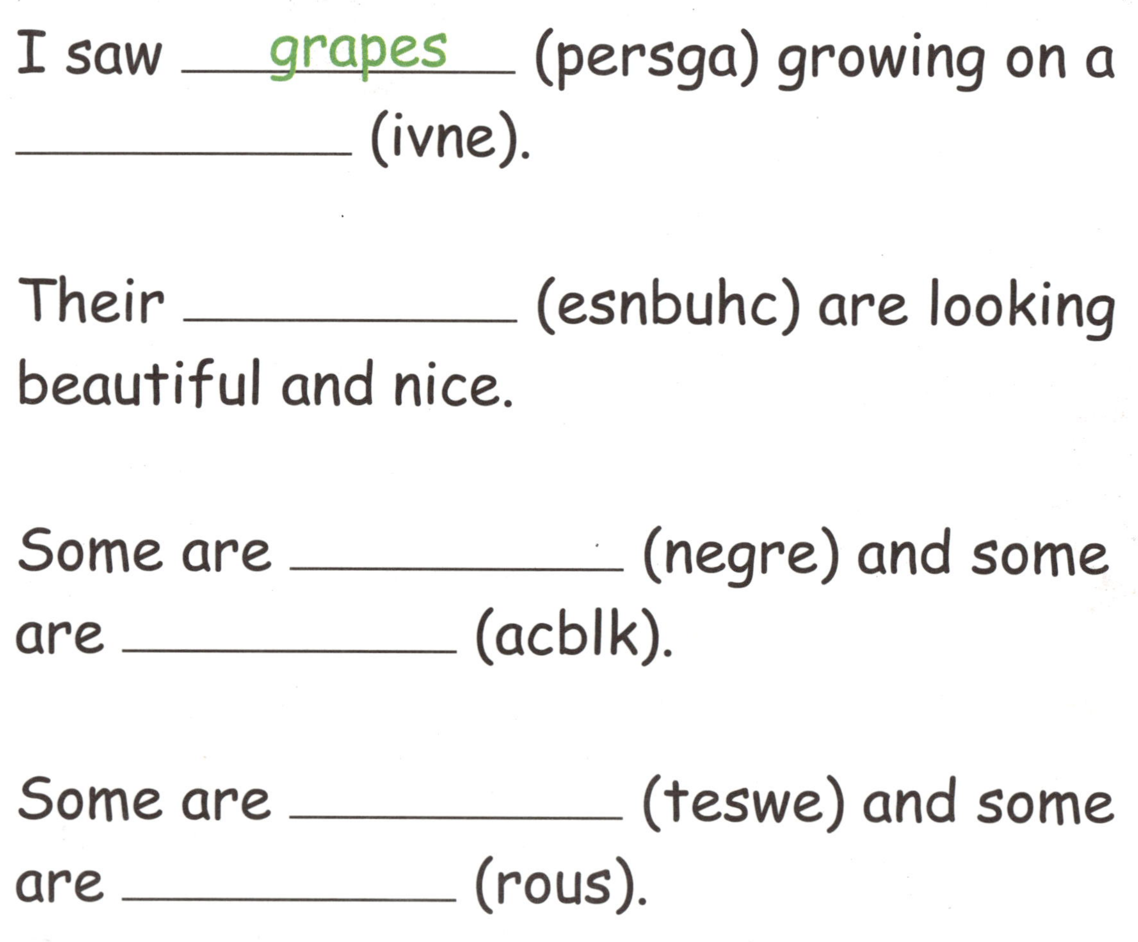

I saw ___grapes___ (persga) growing on a ____________ (ivne).

Their ____________ (esnbuhc) are looking beautiful and nice.

Some are ____________ (negre) and some are ____________ (acblk).

Some are ____________ (teswe) and some are ____________ (rous).

Everyone loves to ____________ (tea) them.

BUTTERFLIES IN THE SKY

Form words that begin with the letters on the butterflies.

How many words do you know?

ri

ODD PICK

Tick (✓) the odd one out in the groups given below.

If you know which one doesn't fit, you will know which one to tick!

mango

potato ✓

lychee

pear

bus

car

boat

scooter

oven

computer

laptop

tablet

dog

cat

cow

tiger

WHO'S IN THE WATER?

Jig went to the beach and saw something interesting. He has written a coded message about it. Can you decode it?

1	2	3	4	5	6	7	8	9	10	11	12	13	14	15
A	D	E	H	I	L	N	O	P	R	S	T	U	Y	W

4 13 10 10 1 14 / 5 / 11 1 15

H __ __ __ __ __ ! / __ / __ __ __

1 / 2 8 6 9 4 5 7 / 5 7

__ / __ __ __ __ __ __ __ / __ __

12 4 3 / 15 1 12 3 10

__ __ __ / __ __ __ __ __ .

PATTERN TIME

Can you complete these letter patterns?

This should be easy, if you remember the alphabet.

ABC CDE D E F EFG FGH

PP __ __ RR SS TT

IJ KL MN __ __ QR

__ __ D4 E5 F6 G7

ZY XW VU TS __ __

TREAT YOURSELF

Help Saw fill in the blanks with the correct words.

The words given in the box will help.

basket   scoop   glass   cup   slice   pack   bunch

Give me a ____slice____ of cake.

Give me a ____________ of grapes.

Give me a ____________ of biscuits.

Give me a ____________ of tea.

Give me a ____________ of milk.

Give me a ____________ of fruits.

Give me a ____________ of ice cream.

WHAT'S IN THE WORD?

Read the big words and find the smaller words in them.

A word with another word in it is called a kangaroo word.

catch ______

action ______

person ______

earth

ear

bold ______

island ______

history ______

WORD BOUQUET

Complete the word bouquet by finding smaller words from the bigger words.

Look for the smaller words in each word.

garden — den

pastry — ______

balloon — ______

cartoon — ______

teacher — ______

swing — ______

SPELLING BEE

Are you a spelling bee? Prove it by writing the correct spellings.

Word	Correct spelling	Word	Correct spelling
plet	plate	truk	
forc		nale	
cyube		trane	
botel		horce	
blak		hypo	

CLIMB THE LADDER

Arrange the words in the alphabetical order, starting from the top rung.

Sing the alphabet song as you sort the words.

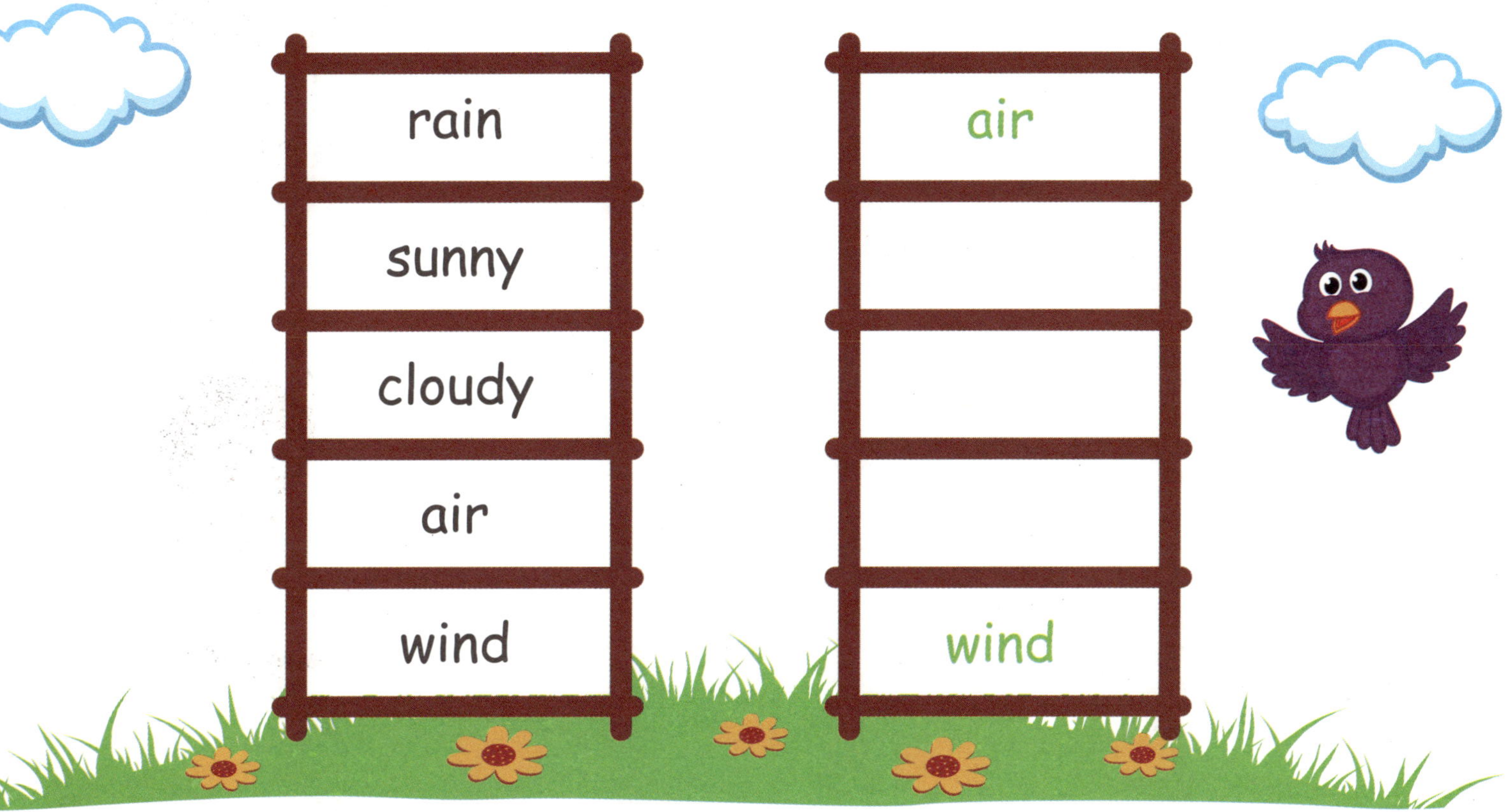

HOW ARE YOU?

Choose the right words from the options to complete these sentences.

The pictures hold the key!

I am a ______caring______ doctor.

smart   caring   greedy

I am a ____________ boy.

dry   shiny   smart

I am a ____________ fox.

brown   black   blue

I am a ____________ owl.

white   brown   green

I am a ____________________ animal.

big   small   tiny

I am a ____________________ soldier.

brave   smart   scared

I am a ____________________ girl.

pretty   big   soft

I am a ____________________ bird.

black   colourful   white

I am a ____________________ animal.

short   round   tall

HE AND SHE

What is the opposite gender?
Fill in the boxes.

king	queen

father	

boy	

lion	

uncle	

hen	

WHAT'S THE MOOD?

These are pictures of Robbie with different expressions. Can you identify his mood in each?

Try to imitate Robbie's expressions.

He is crying.

He is ____________.

He is ____________.

He is ____________.

He is ____________.

He is ____________.

SOUND POPS

Read the words in the balloons aloud. Colour the balloons pink if the words have the "s" sound and yellow if the words have the "k" sound.

Read the words aloud clearly and slowly to know what sounds they are producing.

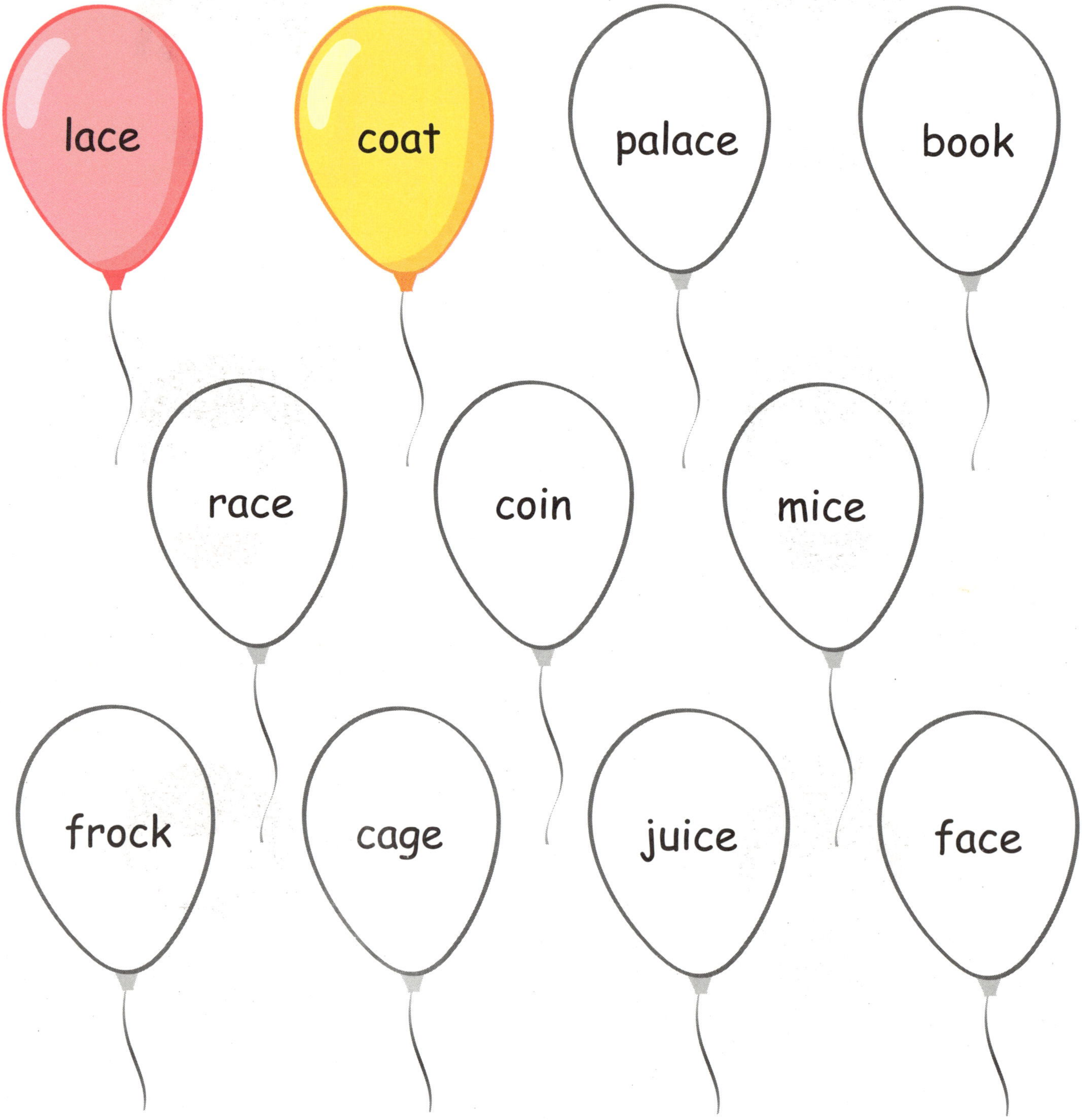

lace

coat

palace

book

race

coin

mice

frock

cage

juice

face

LARGE IS BIG

Help Tina match the words that mean the same.

Can you use each pair in the same sentence? Challenge your friends!

damp •	• duty
quick •	• delete
rough •	• giant
pain •	• desire
crave •	• moist
erase •	• fast
job •	• ache
huge •	• harsh

HOT AND COLD

Pick out the opposites of the first word in each row by colouring the circle green.

You already know what opposites are.

difficult	hard	easy	little
little	young	heavy	big
hot	cold	warm	boiling
giant	tiny	huge	enormous
mute	quiet	silent	loud
evil	bad	wicked	nice
pretty	ugly	smart	beautiful

WORDY CLOUDS

Add "un-" or "dis-" to the beginning of each word to make a new word.

"Un-" and "dis-" are called prefixes. When prefixes are added to words, new words are formed. It is like magic, isn't it?

un + happy = unhappy

+ like =

+ equal =

+ respect =

+ kind =

+ honest =

WHO AM I?

Add -er/-or at the end of each word to form the name of an occupation.

"Er-" and "or-" are suffixes. Suffixes are added at the end of words to form new words.

act + or = actor

teach + ______ = ______________________

paint + ______ = ______________________

doct + ______ = ______________________

sing + ______ = ______________________

farm + ______ = ______________________

SUPER SAIL

Tick (✓) the boat that you want to ride in.

This is an ice cream.

This stops a car.

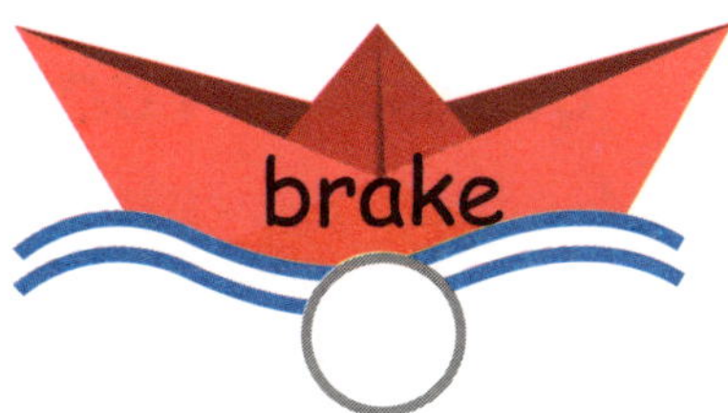

This is a grain.

This is a sweet dish.

The opposite of tight.

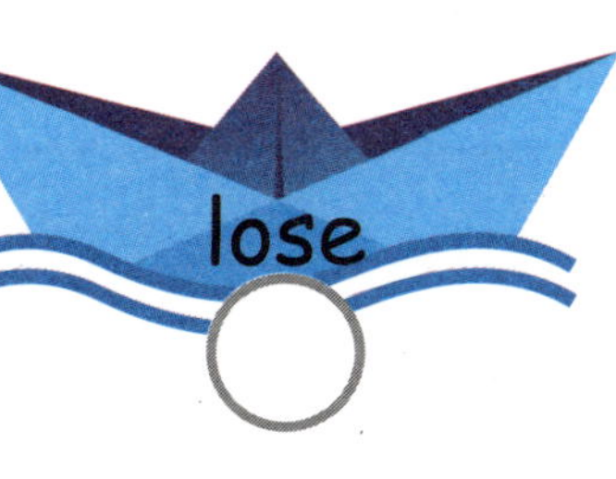

SENTENCE JUMBLE

All the sentences are jumbled. Help Jig set them right.

Always remember that a sentence begins with a capital letter and ends with a full stop.

sky	the	pilot	in	aeroplane	flies	the	an

The pilot flies an aeroplane in the sky.

breakfast	Rahul	bread	for	eats	butter	and

____

family	with	Tina	Kolkata	her	lives	in

____

doctor	My	is	father	a

____

going	I	picnic	am	tomorrow	a	for

____

BUILD A WORD

Saw is putting together bricks to form bigger words. Help her.

Add two words to make a bigger word.

bull | water | back | air | ground

foot | suit | melon | pack | print

plane | play | case | dog

water	melon

TARGET SHOOTING

Cross the balloon with a word that does not rhyme with the others in the row.

Say the words aloud. If the ending sounds match, the words rhyme.

book	hook	cook	~~tooth~~	look
sleep	sheep	deep	deer	beep
draw	claw	paw	straw	bow
mug	buy	bug	tug	jug

SCRATCH YOUR BRAIN

Read the first word relation and select the correct word for the second one.

We use analogies to compare things.

child : teeth : : bird : beak

feather | beak | tail

gloves : hands : : socks : ______

legs | feet | head

cherries : red : : pears : ______

green | purple | white

eyes : see : : nose : ______

hear | walk | smell

fire : hot : : ice : ______

cold | warm | sweet

HUNGRY BUNNY

Circle the carrots that complete the analogies.

Put on your thinking cap.

Bricks make a wall, just as pages make a ____.

 car  map  book  bag

Plumbers repair taps, just as cobblers repair ____.

 bags  laptop  heater  shoes

Days make a week, just as months make a ____.

 hour  time  year  seconds

A triangle has three sides, just as a square has ____.

 five  four  two  six

Birds fly, just as fish ____.

 run  drink  swim  wash

KNOW YOUR SPORT

All these children are playing different sports. Do you know which one?

Do you know the names of different sports? Which one is your favourite?

s	w	i	m	m	i	n	g

		a		i		g

b		d		i		t		

	o		k		y

f		o		b		l	l

	r		c		e	

GOOD MANNERS!

Help Saw learn some good manners.
Tick (✓) the right response.

Do you have good manners?

When your best friend gives you a gift, you say:

- Sorry ◯
- Excuse me ◯
- Thank you ✓
- Wow ◯

When you meet someone, you say:

- Please ◯
- Hello ◯
- Sorry ◯
- Thank you ◯

When you disturb someone, you say:

- Sorry ◯
- Thanks ◯
- Excuse me ◯
- May I? ◯

When you ask for permission, you say:

- May I? ◯
- Good-bye ◯
- Hello ◯
- Please ◯

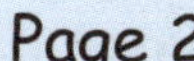

ANSWERS

Page 2

Name a fruit that begins with the fourth vowel.
orange

Which letter sounds like the name of body organ?
I

Which letter sounds like the name of an insect?
B

Which letter sounds like the name of a vegetable?
P

Which letter sounds like the name of a tool?
X

Which letter sounds like the name given to a group of people standing in a line?
Q

Page 3

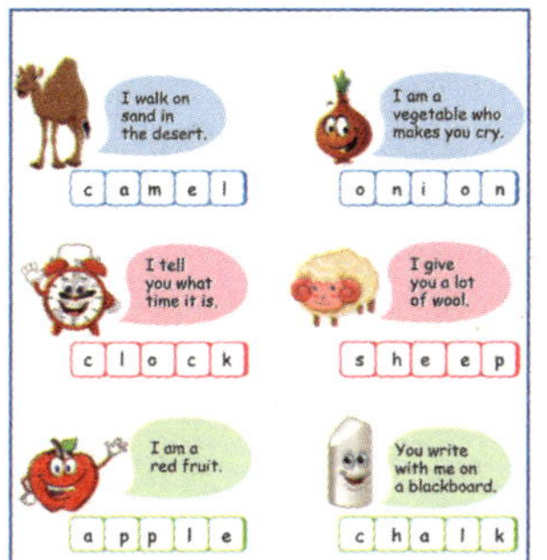

Page 4

I saw grapes (persga) growing on a vine (ivne).

Their bunches (esnbuhc) are looking beautiful and nice.

Some are green (negre) and some are black (acblk).

Some are sweet (teswe) and some are sour (rous).

Children love to eat (tea) them more.

Page 5

For this activity, the answers will vary.

Page 6

Page 7

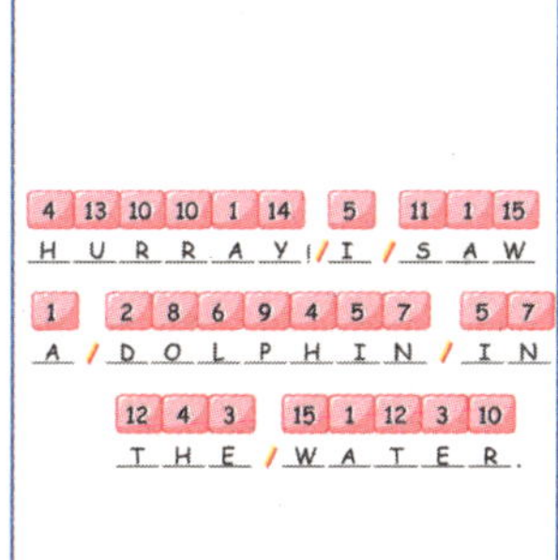

Page 8

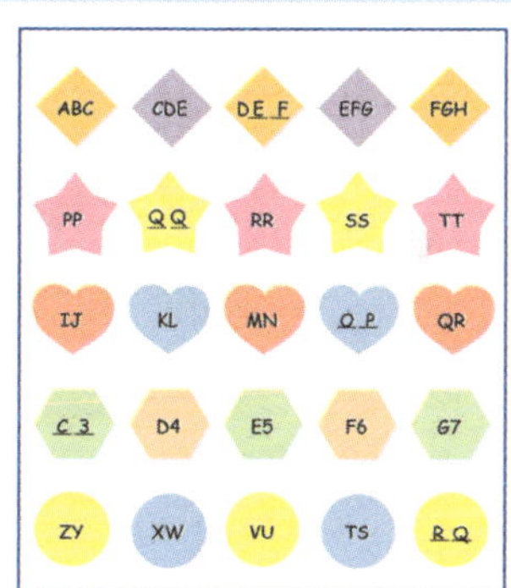

Page 9

Page 10

For this activity, the answers will vary.

Page 11

For this activity, the answers will vary.

Page 12

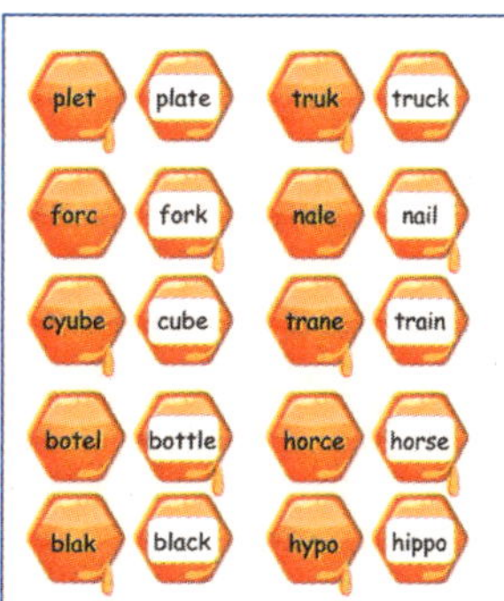

Page 13

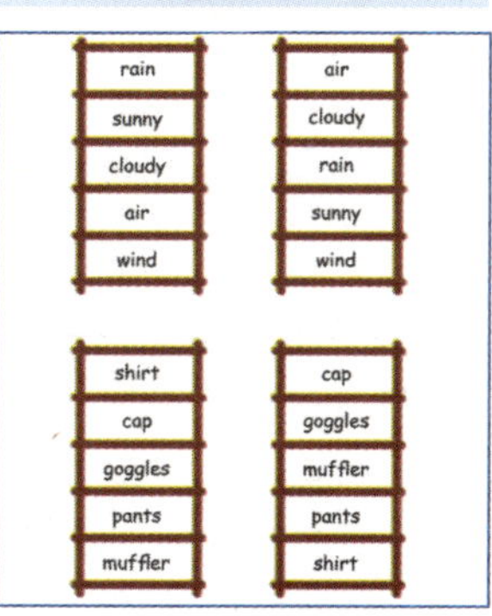

Page 14

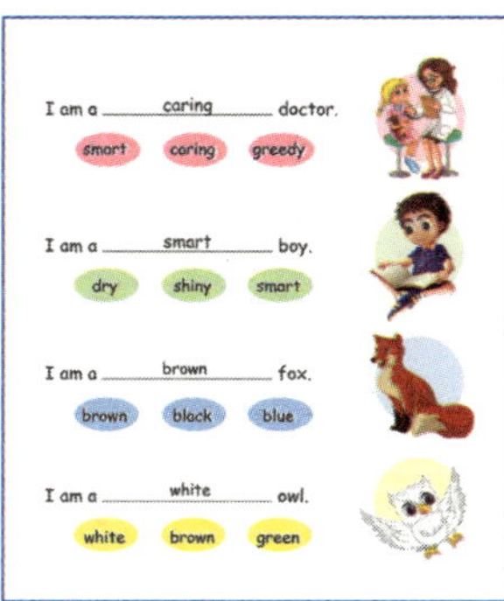

Page 15

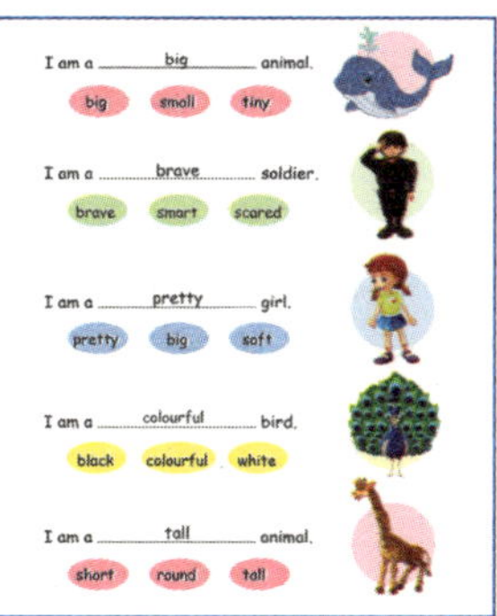

Page 16

Page 17

ANSWERS

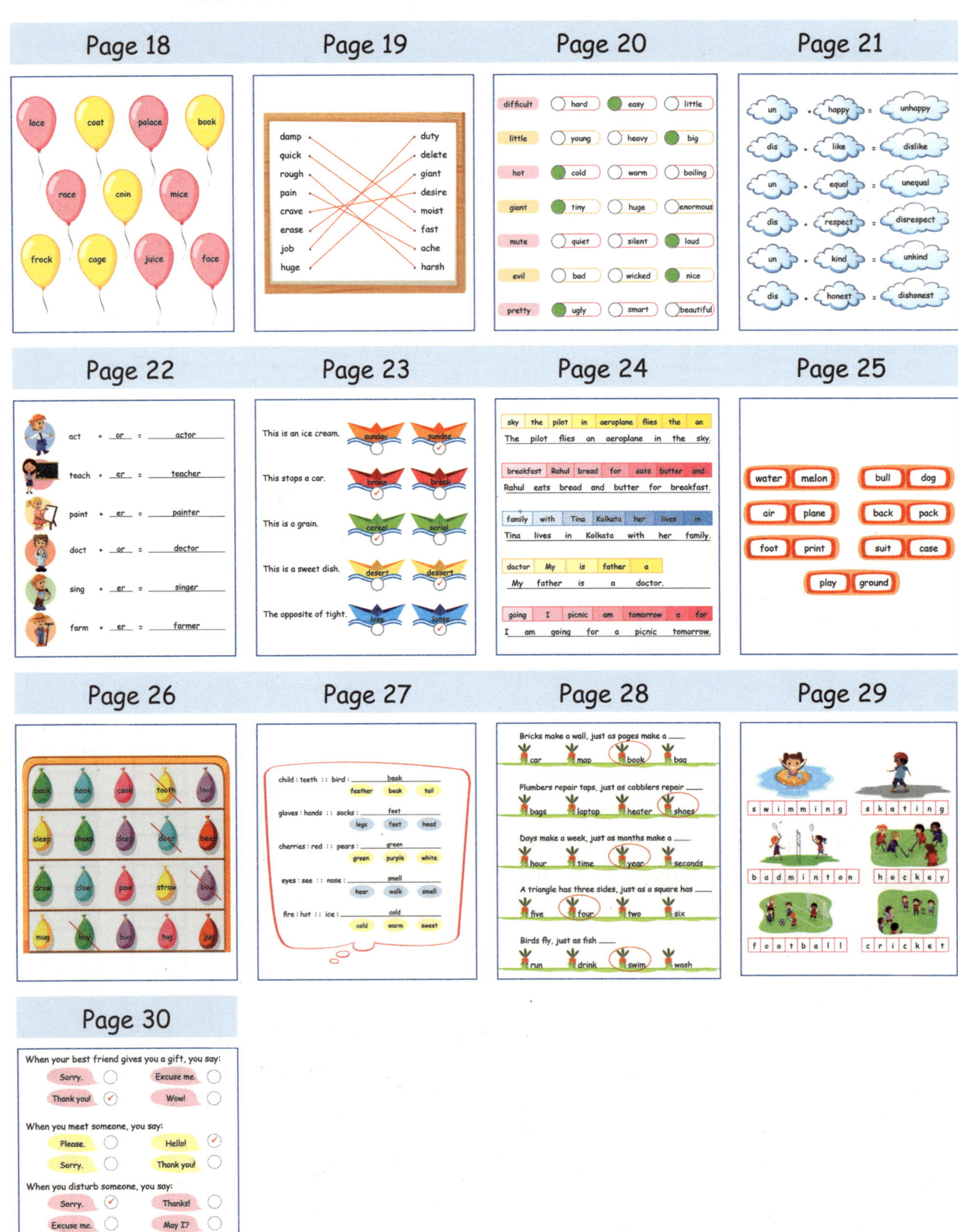
Page 18
lace
coat
palace
book
race
coin
mice
frock
cage
juice
face
Page 19
damp
quick
rough
pain
crave
erase
job
huge
duty
delete
giant
desire
moist
fast
ache
harsh
Page 20
difficult hard easy little
little young heavy big
hot cold warm boiling
giant tiny huge enormous
mute quiet silent loud
evil bad wicked nice
pretty ugly smart beautiful
Page 21
un + happy = unhappy
dis + like = dislike
un + equal = unequal
dis + respect = disrespect
un + kind = unkind
dis + honest = dishonest
Page 22
act + or = actor
teach + er = teacher
paint + er = painter
doct + or = doctor
sing + er = singer
farm + er = farmer
Page 23
This is an ice cream. sunday sundae
This stops a car. brake break
This is a grain. cereal serial
This is a sweet dish. desert dessert
The opposite of tight. lose loose
Page 24
sky the pilot in aeroplane flies the an
The pilot flies an aeroplane in the sky.
breakfast Rahul bread for eats butter and
Rahul eats bread and butter for breakfast.
family with Tina Kolkata her lives in
Tina lives in Kolkata with her family.
doctor My is father a
My father is a doctor.
going I picnic am tomorrow a for
I am going for a picnic tomorrow.
Page 25
water melon
bull dog
air plane
back pack
foot print
suit case
play ground
Page 26
book hook cook tooth look
sleep sheep deep deer beep
draw claw paw straw bow
mug buy bug tug jug
Page 27
child : teeth : : bird : beak
feather beak tail
gloves : hands : : socks : feet
legs feet head
cherries : red : : pears : green
green purple white
eyes : see : : nose : smell
hear walk smell
fire : hot : : ice : cold
cold warm sweet
Page 28
Bricks make a wall, just as pages make a ......
car map book bag
Plumbers repair taps, just as cobblers repair ......
bags laptop heater shoes
Days make a week, just as months make a ......
hour time year seconds
A triangle has three sides, just as a square has ......
five four two six
Birds fly, just as fish ......
run drink swim wash
Page 29
s w i m m i n g
s k a t i n g
b a d m i n t o n
h o c k e y
f o o t b a l l
c r i c k e t
Page 30
When your best friend gives you a gift, you say:
Sorry.
Excuse me.
Thank you!
Wow!
When you meet someone, you say:
Please.
Hello!
Sorry.
Thank you!
When you disturb someone, you say:
Sorry.
Thanks!
Excuse me.
May I?
When you ask for permission, you say:
May I?
Good-bye!
Hello!
Please.